How to REKINDLE THAT SPARK —

and create the relationship and intimacy that you want

— A Life Guide —

How to REKINDLE THAT SPARK —

and create the relationship and intimacy that you want

— A Life Guide —

Created by
DR. SUZANNE GELB, PhD, JD

FIRST EDITION

All rights reserved. This book or any portion thereof may not be reproduced or used in any manner whatsoever without the express written permission of the publisher except for the use of brief quotations in a book review.

Copyright © 2019 Dr. Suzanne J. Gelb, Ph.D., J.D.

Manufactured in the United States of America.

ISBN-13: 978-1-950764-12-9
ISBN-10: 1-950764-12-5

www.DrSuzanneGelb.com

PRAISE FOR... THE LIFE GUIDES

The author wrote this life guide on how to rekindle that spark — and create the relationship and intimacy [sex life][1] that you want, as well as 10 other life guides on various topics, to help readers successfully navigate some of life's trickiest challenges.

Each Life Guide includes educational information sourced from the author's three-plus decades of coaching and counseling in the field of emotional wellness.

What Readers Are Saying

"This Guide got us out of our relationship rut and helped us stir up the passion we felt early on in our relationship, and to remember why we fell in love in the first place.

Thanks to the simple and do-able exercises, we have revived fun, play and touch in our relationship. Hand-holding and hugs used to be a thing of the past. No more!"

—J and E

"Before working through this Guide, we were more like roommates who've lived together for years and the romance had gone. Thanks to this Guide we share much more affection and connection, and my lingerie is no longer collecting dust!

We are also more compassionate and kind to each other. And now we schedule time for each other — even if it's for sex. We have to

---

[1] In this Life Guide, "intimacy" and "sex life" are used interchangeably.

reserve this time, and we look forward to sharing an activity together."

—R and J

"We were contemplating divorce. Then we thought we'd 'try one last time' ... so we read your guide. Now? We're best friends again, off-the-top lovers, and totally recommitted.

PS. We're not exaggerating. Dr. Gelb's Life Guide is amazing. It works!"

—M and N

"Your guidebooks are gems."

—Alexandra Franzen, Published Author, Writing Teacher

"Learning how to love yourself and treat yourself kindly — even when your life, career, body, and relationships aren't 'totally perfect' — is one of the hardest things to do.

Dr. Suzanne Gelb breaks down the art of self-love into practical steps. No woo-woo vagueness. Just easy-to-follow exercises pulled from her 28-year career in the field.

If you're looking for practicality and effectiveness, these Life Guides are a steal of a deal."

—Susan Hyatt, Master Certified Life Coach, Published Author

"Dr. Gelb has a gentle spirit that instantly makes you feel like you've come home. The depth of her wisdom is undeniable, her

curiosity is insatiable and her love is palpable. These qualities make her the perfect guide for life.

In the pages of the Life Guides you will find practical and proven processes to support you in living your great life.

Whether it's heart-centered wisdom on navigating the dating world, love-based strategies for becoming a parent, or reaching your ideal weight through kindness, Dr. Gelb's Life Guides are gifts to be treasured."

—Dr. Gemma Stone, psychologist

CONTENTS

Disclaimer.   xv

INTRODUCTION

You Started This Relationship Together, You Can
Nourish and Improve It Together.   1

WHAT'S INSIDE
AND HOW TO USE THIS GUIDE   8

STEP 1

Write Down Your Feelings.   9

STEP 2

Release Negative Feelings ... Safely.   15

STEP 3

Say What You Want.   23

STEP 4

Write a New Commitment.   29

STEP 5

Play ... Touch ... Kiss ... Date! 7 Days of Spark.   36

Happy Endings: 3 Couples Who Rekindled the Spark,
After all Hope Seemed Lost.

STEP 6

Release Expectations. 66

WRAP UP

It Is Possible To Grow, and To Love Again. 69

MORE TIPS, MORE TOOLS

FAQs About Decreased Sex Drive — Causes and Fixes. ... 71

WHAT'S NEXT?

Resources… To Keep the "Spark" Shining. 81

ABOUT THE AUTHOR 95

OTHER BOOKS BY THE AUTHOR 96

INDEX 98

DISCLAIMER

This book is a tool that can help you learn how to rekindle that "spark" with your partner — and create the relationship and intimacy that you want.

This book contains educational exercises and tips drawn from my career in the field of emotional wellness with over 30 years of experience. This book is for informational purposes only, and is not intended to diagnose or treat any illness, nor is it a substitute for professional or psychological advice, diagnosis, or treatment. Always consult a qualified health care professional before engaging in any new, self-help resource (such as this one) and with questions you may have about your health and wellbeing.

Any case material that may be alluded to in this book, including in articles, or in interviews [see Resources section] does not constitute guarantees of similar outcomes for the reader. No results can be promised, since everyone's personal development path is unique. Names and details have been changed for privacy.

Links inside this book to external websites are for informational purposes only. Linking does not imply endorsement of or affiliation with that site, its content, or any product or service it may offer.

All link URLs in this book are current at the time of printing. Link URLs may fail at some point if the page has been deleted or moved. The author assumes no responsibility or liability for broken links.

This concludes the disclaimer portion of this book.

Enjoy the Life Guide. Here's to loving, sexy, happy relationships.

INTRODUCTION

You Started This Relationship Together, You Can Nourish and Improve It Together.

Welcome to the Life Guide on How To Rekindle That "Spark" With Your Partner and Create the Relationship and Intimacy [Sex Life][2] That You Want.

If you picked up a copy of this Guide, chances are, you might be feeling ...

— **Seriously annoyed ...**

with your partner.

("I can barely stand to LOOK at him right now, let alone want to have SEX with him!")

---

[2] In this Life Guide, "intimacy" and "sex life" are used interchangeably.

— **Seriously annoyed ...**

with yourself.

("I've allowed myself to get so stressed out and exhausted. It's my fault we never have sex anymore.")

— **Ashamed**

at how "bad" things have gotten.

("It's literally been ... months. Are we a hopeless case?")

— **Guilty**

for not taking better care of yourself.

("I've put on weight ... I haven't been tending to my appearance. No wonder he / she's lost interest in me.")

— **Disinterested**

in intimacy and sex,

or

— **Disconnected**

from what turns you on.

("My ultimate 'fantasy'? Umm, I don't know ... maybe a bag of potato chips, and some peace and quiet?")

— Just plain **hopeless.**

("I just don't know if we can work this out...")

You're not alone.

When I work with couples where one or both partners lack interest in sex and intimacy, I often hear things like:

"I love my wife, but for years she's had no desire to be intimate.

How long do I let my marriage continue without intimacy?"

Or:

"I've been married for several years, but I'm afraid my husband and I won't ever be intimate again.

Why do I have low libido?"

These people are experiencing a problem that impacts a lot of relationships, yet it's one that many are reluctant to talk about:

low libido, or loss of desire.

Since physical intimacy is a meaningful part of a relationship, loss of desire can seriously affect your partnership.

Regardless of who lacks interest… whether it's:

— one partner,

or

— both,

the result tends to be the same.

There is an absence of physical contact, which one or both partners may experience as a form of "rejection."

**WHAT IS "INTIMACY" ANYWAY?
(AND WHAT'S "NORMAL"?)**

Physical intimacy includes:

— sensuous

and

— sexual

activity between two people,

and the sharing of:

— responses,

— thoughts

and

— feelings

related to these activities.

It can be anything from:

— holding your partner's hand ...

to

— giving a quick squeeze on your way off to work ...

to

— cuddling ...

to

— having sex ...

and

— everything in between.

There is no "magic number" that indicates how much intimacy is "healthy" or "correct."

What matters is that both of you feel connected to one another, deeply loved and satisfied.

LOSS OF DESIRE: HOW IT HAPPENS.

Loss of desire can be so **painful** and **frustrating**.

Often, couples are left wondering:

"How did this happen?"

There are many factors that can contribute to low libido, or loss of desire.

Sometimes, these factors are **emotional**.

For example, pent-up feelings of:

— frustration,

— anger,

— jealousy

or even

— self-loathing,

that may be festering inside.

Other times, these factors can be **lifestyle-based**.

For example, being:

— too busy,

— too rushed,

and / or

— not creating the time and space needed to:

- slow down

and

- connect.

At other times, these factors are **physical**.

For example, possibly caused by:

— an under-active thyroid

or

— the side effects of medication, for starters.

Sometimes, it's a **combination of several factors** — or all of the above!

It's always wise to consult your physician to uncover any physiological factors that might be affecting your libido, so all the bases are covered.

Once those physical factors have been addressed (if they were an issue), then it becomes easier to pinpoint which **emotional** and **lifestyle** aspects (if any) may need attention.

What's Inside and How To Use This Guide

Inside this Life Guide, you'll find a series of 6 steps to help you rekindle that "spark" with your partner, and create the relationship and sex life that you want.

HOW TO GIVE THIS GUIDE THE BEST CHANCE TO WORK FOR YOUR RELATIONSHIP:

It's important for both of you to read and work through this Guide, together.

You **started** this relationship **together**,

and that's why it's so **important** that you:

— **nourish**

and

— **improve it**,

together.

The Contents page of this Life Guide gave you a peek at what's ahead.

STEP 1

Write Down Your Feelings.

As a psychologist and life coach, I almost always begin my sessions with clients with a simple emotional "check-in" to support them to get in touch with their feelings.

Why start there?

Because…

Pent-up, unresolved feelings may be the very thing that's holding you back from enjoying more intimacy with your partner.

It's not easy to release these emotions if…

— you aren't really aware of which feelings are interfering, to begin with.

WRITING EXERCISE

You can start here, with a writing exercise to get all those feelings out on the page.

It's best if both of you complete this exercise separately — each writing on your own sheet of paper.

Later, you can **share** some of your answers with one another.

(More on that in a moment.)

A few pointers, before you begin:

If possible, **write** your answers on a piece of paper, **by hand** — you're likely to find that this process tends to slow you down, giving you **time to think**.

The benefit?

You're **more involved** with what you're writing, instead of (as is the case with many people):

— typing quickly

and not always staying:

— focused on,

or being thoroughly

— attentive to,

what you're writing.

Try not to:

— over-think your answers

or

— worry

if they sound:

— "positive"

or

— "negative"

or even

— "irrational"
or

— "silly."

Let go of any self-criticism.

That also means disregard:

— spelling and punctuation

and, resist any temptation to:

— edit

Just give yourself permission to express whatever you feel.

Take as much time and space as you want, to complete your writing.

FILL IN THE BLANKS:

When I look at my body, I feel

_____

_____

_____

_____

When I look at my partner's body, I feel

_____

_____

_____

_____

When I think about kissing my partner, I feel

_____

_____

_____

_____

When I think about having sex with my partner, I feel

_____

_____

_____

_____

I'm so tired of trying (and not succeeding) to

_____

_____

_____

I'm so mad at myself for

_____

_____

_____

This whole situation makes me feel

STEP 2

Release Negative Feelings ... Safely.

Have you ever noticed what very young children often do when they're frustrated or need something?

Sitting in their crib, they'll:

— pound their little hands and feet on the mattress,

and probably

— make some sounds to express how they feel,

and

— hopefully get their caregiver's attention.

Once the child is done pounding, invariably, he (or she) is **calmer** because **their frustration has been released!**

AN EXERCISE FOR EMOTIONAL RELEASE

The following exercise is essentially the young child version of "pounding your crib," but adapted for adults.

According to my research, as well as my professional experience with clients over many years, this process can be **incredibly effective — a powerful form of emotional release**.

At this point, it's best for each of you to do this exercise **alone**, in a safe, private space — not together as a couple.

HERE'S HOW IT'S DONE:

1. Knot up one end of a hand towel,

2. Grab a pillow

and

3. Retreat to a safe, private space, like:

    - a home office,
    - den,
    - bathroom

or

    - a garage with a lock on the door.

Then…

4. Pound the pillow with the knotted end of the towel

while

5. Verbalizing your feelings, out loud.

LOTS OF FEELINGS... WHERE TO START?

You can start with the **anger you're feeling**, **towards yourself**:

Self, I'm so mad at you for

_____

_____

_____

_____

Then, you can express your **anger as it relates to your partner**:

[Partner's name]

_____

I'm so mad at you for

_____

_____

_____

_____

REMEMBER:

Any feelings that you express during this exercise, must **only** be directed towards the pillow that you're pounding. These feelings must **not** be directed or expressed towards any person.

This is because this pillow-pounding exercise is intended to be a safe and effective vehicle for you to **release your intense, pent-up emotions,** in a way that doesn't harm:

— yourself (physically or emotionally), someone else, or the environment.

That is the reason why you:

— express your pent-up emotions **only** towards an appropriate, inanimate object (e.g., a pillow),

and why you:

— **do not** express these pent-up emotions towards any person or object.

For example:

Say you're frustrated because your laptop's not working properly. It would **not** be appropriate — out of total frustration — to angrily slam down the lid of the laptop, and possibly damage the device, or cause it to malfunction (I've heard from more than one person, that this was their experience.)

Now… back to the exercise.

HOW LONG DOES THIS POUNDING EXERCISE TAKE?

Keep

— pounding

and

— repeating the pounding,

until you feel…

— a sense of **emotional release**.

(More on that in a moment.)

WHAT IF IT'S "TOO NOISY?"

You **don't** have to:

— yell at the top of your lungs

or

— pound so intensely

that…

— you build your biceps!

But if you're concerned about noise levels, if feasible, you might try …

— Turning up the radio or TV,

— going into the bathroom and running the shower. (Water tends to absorb sound),

— making sure that everyone is out of the house, to set your mind at ease

and / or

— having a conversation with the people who share your home with you, and explaining that this pounding exercise is a good thing — a healthy way to release pent-up feelings.

You might even choose:

— a designated "**venting zone**" in your home, where anyone in your family (or your roommate/s), who wants to, can go whenever they need to release some pent-up, negative emotions.

Again ...

However and wherever you choose to do this pillow-pounding exercise, the point is to **keep expressing how you feel**, and **keep pounding that pillow**, until you feel **a sense of emotional relief**.

WHAT "EMOTIONAL RELIEF" FEELS LIKE.

When you're done with your pounding, you might feel:

— **a sense of peace**.

You may find that you want to:

— have **a deep, long cry**.

You might feel:

— quite **drained**, but in a **good** way...

like:

— you've just **unloaded a heavy burden,**

and now

— you're experiencing the **fatigue** from having carried that load.

(If that's the case, **give yourself permission to rest** a bit.)

These can all be good signs that you've released some pent-up emotions.

If you're still feeling strong emotions, it doesn't mean that:

— you did the pillow-pounding exercise "wrong,"

or that:

— it wasn't effective.

It just means that:

There is more emotional energy to release, safely — when you are ready.

It's like peeling an onion.

One layer at a time.

Now that the two of you have **safely released** some **pent-up feelings**, you're ready to:

— have a **calm, productive conversation**

about:

— **the kind of relationship you want,**

instead of:

— "going numb"

or

— lashing out in frustration.

Ready?

Let's move on to Step 3!

STEP 3

Say What You Want.

People who have enjoyed a strong, sexy spark with each other in the past, and pleasurable intimacy, **don't just "lose the spark" for no reason.**

Something's getting in the way of what you both want — often, several "somethings."

Some partners may be harboring:

— hurt feelings

or

— resentment.

Some are preoccupied with:

— work

or

— family demands.

Perhaps, something was:

— lacking all along (possibly a deeper emotional connection, not just 'great sex'). But that 'lack' is only just now coming to the surface.

Some people are embarrassed:

— to talk about sex and desire, period.

(Which means there's a strong possibility that they're inhibited in the bedroom, also.) Somehow this hasn't been an issue. Until now.

THE OUTCOME:

One or both partners "get used" to having no libido. And their relationship is more like a "roommate" situation.

In this step of this Life Guide, you'll be invited to:

have a conversation about what might be getting in the way of you enjoying the relationship and sex life that you want.

But, before we get into that:

What DO you want, anyway?

It may seem like an overly simplistic question, but it's worth exploring together, especially if:

— it's **not** something you've talked about openly, for a while!

START BY HAVING A CONVERSATION, TOGETHER.

Try not to let:

— embarrassment

("I couldn't say that, I'd sound so silly...")

or

— self-criticism

("You're acting like a teenager!")

hold you back from saying what you really WANT to say.

Try to allow yourself to:

— **speak** from your heart,

— **feel** worthy of expressing what you desire,

and

— **know** that you deserve to be treated with love and respect.

Take turns completing the following statements out loud:

I would love to give affection to you by

_____

_____

_____

_____

I would love to receive affection from you by

_____

_____

_____

_____

Some of the things that make me feel sexy / spark-y / excited to connect and be intimate are

_____

_____

_____

_____

Some of the things that dampen those spark-y feelings are

_____

_____

_____

_____

When it comes to sex and intimacy, one of my fantasies is

_____

_____

_____

_____

When it comes to sex and intimacy, one of my preferences is

_____

_____

_____

_____

After sharing this kind of conversation, you're likely to be a bit clearer about

- **what's getting in the way of the intimacy that you want... the things that are dampening that spark...**

as well as

- **the kind of relationship and sharing you're both striving to create.**

NEXT:

You and your partner get to write a new commitment to yourselves and each other.

A commitment of:

- **renewed connection,**

- **affection**

and

- **care.**

AND AFTER THAT?

We'll explore **how to bring back that spark in practical ways.**

(Get ready for seven days of touching, kissing and appreciation — with simple rituals and practices to try, every day!)

STEP 4

Write a New Commitment.

When you create a new business partnership, commit to paying off a loan, take on a new job, or choose a new goal, what's the first thing that you generally do?

Put it in writing.

It's no wonder that our society relies on written contracts, so heavily.

Putting things in writing tends to make us significantly more likely to follow through.

Ever wonder why so many people make "To Do" lists? Perhaps you're one of those people.

If so, ask yourself:

"Why do I make these lists?"

Your answer is likely to be something along these lines:

"I'm more likely to achieve my goals if I write them down. I'm more likely to get things done."

So,

when it comes to creating a new kind of relationship, it's very powerful to get your new commitment down on paper.

To create your new commitment, start by:

WRITING DOWN A LIST OF THINGS THAT YOU ARE NOT GOING TO DO ANY LONGER.

You can:

— copy the following phrases onto a fresh sheet of paper, verbatim,

or

— you can adjust the words so that they make more sense for your situation.

Add as many NOT's as you like, until you both feel complete.

It's a good idea for you and your partner to complete this exercise at the same time.

So pick a time when **both of you can be together**, each writing your own list **by hand**, on a separate sheet of paper.

I am NOT going to:

- let my frustration about my partner build up and fester inside me, so that I'm turned off from desiring sex.

I am NOT going to:

- engage in sex because I feel "I have to" — making it feel like a chore or an obligation.

  I am going to engage because I want to.

I am NOT going to:

- cling to past hurts and frustrations.

  I will forgive my partner for saying hurtful things to me, and forgive myself for saying hurtful things to him / her.

I am NOT going to:

- ignore my own desires.

  I will make a conscious effort to be attentive and sensitive to my desires, and express what I want.

I am NOT going to:

- pack my schedule so tightly that I no longer have time for laughter, conversation, touch and smiles.

When you are both feeling complete, **read your NOT lists out loud to one another**.

If you'd like, you can do a small ritual to release any lingering negativity and clear the way to a new beginning.

Tear up your NOT lists into tiny pieces and toss them into the air, burn them with a candle, or eat them like an international spy (just kidding! Don't do that.)

Then,

shift into positive language.

WRITE DOWN A COMMITMENT ABOUT WHAT YOU <u>WILL</u> DO, BEGINNING RIGHT THIS MOMENT.

Here are some phrases that might resonate with one or both of you.

But, again — **feel free to create your own!**

If something is bothering me, I WILL

- communicate that to my partner — respectfully, without criticism or blame.

I WILL

- make time in my busy schedule for intimacy with my partner.

I WILL

- be more appreciative of my partner and express that appreciation openly.

I WILL

- forgive my partner for saying hurtful things to me in the past.

I WILL

- make a conscious effort to be attentive, sensitive and supportive towards myself and my partner.

I WILL

- help out more, without being asked.

If my desire for intimacy feels frozen, I WILL

- reflect on why that's happened and try to unthaw it.

I WILL

- make sure that I bring laughter and smiles to my relationship.

I WILL

- make touching, kissing, cuddling and sex a priority in my life.

When you are both feeling complete, **read your I WILL lists out loud to one another.**

Perhaps you'll want to:

— "merge" your individual lists into ONE list on a brand-new piece of paper for both of you to date an sign... like a love contract.

Or,

perhaps you'll want to:

—keep your lists entirely separate... each of you focusing on different commitments, in support of the relationship that you share.

Whatever you choose to do ... this time, **don't** burn or tear up your paper.

Instead, put your lists somewhere that you can revisit them, often.

For example:

— tucked into a journal on your bedside table,

— taped up by your bathroom mirror

or

— pinned to a bulletin board in your living room.

When you're both done with this exercise, take a moment to

acknowledge the huge contribution to your relationship that you've just made.

This may be the first time that you've written down (and spoken) a specific commitment to one another, since your wedding day (or the equivalent) ... or maybe, forever!

Take a few deep breaths.

Now could be a good time to:

— hold hands,

— hug,

or

— share some physical touch

and

— eye contact.

Take a moment to savor this special milestone.

Now that you've written a new commitment, it's time for the fun part.

Bringing that commitment into your everyday life, with 7 days of kissing, touching, connection ... and dates!

STEP 5

Play ... Touch ... Kiss ... Date! 7 Days of Spark.

Writing down a new commitment is powerful — but that commitment doesn't amount to much of anything, unless you...

put your words into action.

Here are **7 playful ways** that both of you can start **rekindling** those tingly, sexy feelings.

I call this exercise, **"7 Days of Spark."**

All of the activities are intended for both of you to do, and share, together.

There's a different activity for each one of the 7 days. So, be sure to:

allocate enough time in each of the 7 days, to do an exercise.

Never be too busy to make time to:

— **nurture** your relationship

and

— take your relationship **"to the next level!"**

Investing time, energy and love in your relationship is one of the best investments you can make.

You **don't need to**:

— try all 7 of the exercises,

and,

you **don't need to**:

— flow in the exact order that the exercises are listed.

Just choose whatever exercise feels intriguing... and

give it a whirl!

DAY 1.

Make an "I love when you..." list.

If you only choose ONE thing to try, make it this one.

Over the course of one day, each of you can **make your own list** of everything your partner does that:

- makes you **happy**

and

- **excites** you ("turns you on") ...

even just a tiny bit.

For example:

"I love when you:

- *greet me at the door when I come home from work..."*

"I love when you:

- *stand behind me and give me a hug when I'm washing the dishes..."*

"I love when you:

- *tell me I look beautiful when I'm putting on my work clothes and getting ready to leave for the day..."*

Keep building your separate lists, all day long, even when you're apart.

Then, at the end of the day,

— sit close together

and

— **read both of your lists out loud, to each other.**

DAY 2.

Say "I'm glad that you're here."

... with your **words** AND your **actions**.

Over the course of one day, try to say to your partner,

"[Partner's name], I'm glad that you're here"

at least three times.

You can:

— **say** the words,

and / or

— express yourself through **touch**...,

— a little squeeze

or

— a gentle kiss on the cheek.

Keep expressing your **appreciation**.

Keep letting your partner know, with your words and your actions, that you don't take their presence for granted.

DAY 3.

Make an "It would be amazing if..." list.

Over the course of one day, make a list of everything that you'd LOVE your partner to:

- try doing ...

or

- do more of.

Think of it like an **"ultimate fantasy list."**

"It would be amazing if:

- *I came home from work, and you were waiting in bed. In "almost nothing" lingerie..."*

"It would be amazing if:

- *you called me at 5 pm to say, 'meet me outside.' And then swept me away for a romantic date night..."*

"It would be amazing if:

- *you woke me up with a foot massage, and brought me breakfast in bed..."*

Keep building your separate lists, all day long, even when you're apart.

Then, at the end of the day,

— sit close together

and

— **read both of your lists out loud, to each other**.

EXTRA CREDIT:

— Choose one fantasy scenario, each ...

and

— DO them!

DAY 4.

Try a day of "no intimacy (sex)."

It may seem counter-intuitive, but **try**…

- blocking out a whole day where you're not "allowed" to have sex.

(Ideally, that would be a day when you're both not working.)

Kissing is fine.

Foreplay is fair game.

But…

- no "all-the-way (intercourse)."

Build:

- tension

and

- excitement

like **teenagers** …

Perhaps like:

- you did back when you were first **dating**.

Send each other juicy texts

ALL

DAY

LONG ...

building even more **anticipation** ...

for **your**

BIG

"REUNION"!

Set a **special time** (say, 9 pm) **when you're...**

- "allowed" to have sex again.

Have fun!

DAY 5.

Have a solo date.

Today, create some time for both of you to **enjoy a romantic date ... for one.**

Perhaps **one of you wants to**:

- enjoy a bubble bath

or

- a long, hot shower

and then

- explore

and

- enjoy your own body, alone, at home.

Perhaps **one of you wants to**:

- go out for a beautiful meal,
- do some:journaling,

and

- check into a hotel for a pampering spa treatment.

Whatever you choose to do, pay close attention to how you feel, all throughout your solo date.

Tune into **sensation**:

- what feels

    good

- what feels

    not-so-good

- what feels

    amazing…

so that you can "report back" to your partner, once you reunite.

DAY 6.

Make five kisses a part of today.

One of the most **powerful** ways to energize and nurture a happy marriage or partnership, is by:

feeling "connected" to your spouse or partner...

often,

and in a meaningful way.

How do you establish the "connection?"

It doesn't have to be via:

— candle-light dinners,

or

—exotic vacations (but if you can pull those off, that's great!)...

It can be via something as simple as:

— taking a few seconds as often as possible, during your waking moments, to give each other a **quick**, but **meaningful kiss**.

REMINDER (you probably know this):

It's easy for partners to find themselves on **"automatic"** if they **routinely** give each other a quick:

— *"Goodbye, have a great day,"* peck on the cheek

in the morning as each trots off to work,

or a

— *"Hi, I'm home,"* peck in the evening, when they return.

That **doesn't** tend to establish "connection."

Instead, it tends to be more of a **mindless habit**.

Today, make it a point to enjoy five kisses with your partner.

This doesn't have to:

— "go" anywhere

or

— lead to sexual intercourse.

Just let it be what it is.

Maybe, in the future, you'll decide to:

— make it part of your day, every day!

DAY 7.

Be seen at your best.

A colleague of mine is dating a chef.

She finds him incredibly attractive, all the time, but…

when she has a chance to see him **working** in the kitchen — **his ultimate passion!** — she says:

"His "sexiness" is almost too much to bear!"

Seeing your partner at his or her "best" — engaged in an activity that lights up the soul,

whether it's :

— caring for a child,

— speaking onstage,

— writing,

— cooking,

— teaching,

or

— playing the guitar —

can be wildly attractive.

Today, find a way for:

- **both of you to see one another ...**

    at your personal best.

For example:

Bring your partner to:

- work,
- school,
- the gym,
- the studio where you like to paint ...

wherever you feel like the best version of yourself.

Clear some time later in the day, too ...

Why?

Because after seeing one another at your best, you might really want to have sex!

HAPPY ENDINGS:

3 COUPLES WHO REKINDLED THE SPARK, AFTER ALL HOPE SEEMED LOST.

By this point, after reading (and going through) the first 5 steps in this Life Guide, you and your partner might be feeling:

- hopeful,

- excited ...

and maybe,

- just a little bit doubtful.

"Is all of this stuff really going to help?"

... one of you might be thinking.

"I don't know.

Maybe we're just beyond the point of repair."

... the other might be secretly fearing.

I want to press "pause" before we move on to Step 6, and share three stories about couples whom I've worked with — **couples who really believed that their relationships were doomed**.

These stories can be illustrative of the fact that,

yes,

the tools that you're learning in this Life Guide really can make a difference.

And that,

— **strengthening your bond** with your partner

and

— **creating** a **beautiful kind of intimacy** (sex life)

is possible…

no matter how "gloomy" things may look right now.

JEFF AND VAL:

A story of forgiveness.

When Jeff and Val walk into my office, they've been married for seven years.

Sex?

Not happening.

"Val, you're always criticizing me," Jeff complains.

"You hurt my feelings and then I just don't want to be near you."

Val responds,

"I'm frustrated.

You don't help at home with the kids or appreciate what's involved in running this family."

Val sighs, feeling rejected by Jeff's disinterest.

"I guess I'm not appealing to you, anymore."

In the past, Jeff and Val have made some **sporadic attempts** to rekindle their intimacy, but...

nothing has worked.

They're bitter and angry, but...

hopeful that counseling might help them stay out of divorce court.

In counseling, Jeff and Val quickly learn that:

the desire to have sex (or NOT have sex) can often be an indication of how the rest of the relationship is going.

For example:

Jeff's **disinterest** in sex is linked to:

— the **anger** he feels towards Val.

"She complains I never have time for her," he says.

"She doesn't appreciate the long hours I work to support our family.

We fight over this, but nothing gets resolved.

This angers me and I then don't feel loving or attracted to her."

They learn that:

the key to creating the relationship and sex life that they want ... is forgiveness.

After several counseling sessions, old wounds **begin to heal.**

— Inattention,

— insensitivity

and

— hostility

start to be replaced with:

— **mutual support**.

Jeff begins to feel:

- **happier**

and

- **more committed** to the marriage.

He starts:

- **helping** out at home, without being asked.

Val senses Jeff's new attitude, and responds by:

- giving him **more affection** than he's received in many, many years.

In time, the spark returns.

During one of their final counseling sessions with me, Jeff shares an important insight:

"I'm realizing that for intimacy to be enjoyable, our personal relationship must be healthy.

We have to forgive each other for what's happened in the past.

Clinging to anger is what drove us apart."

Val is pleased to share that:

"With mutual support and caring in place, we are closer than ever before."

Before leaving my office, Jeff makes note of one more important improvement…

He is thrilled to be able to say that:

"Rekindling the spark in our marriage has had a positive impact on our kids, as well."

"That's right," says Val, with a smile.

"Jeff and I now hug in front of them, and the kids see that we love each other. We're helping them to feel more secure."

DON AND MITSI:

Finding the real issues.

When Don and Mitsi meet me for the first time, they've been married for three years.

But you certainly wouldn't know it, watching them interact.

They look more like roommates.

Don asks Mitsi:

"You're not interested in having sex anymore.

Is something wrong?"

Mitsi replies:

"I'm so involved with parenting and work, and you're so busy with work, too.

Sex is the last thing on my mind."

Don responds,

"I understand how busy your days are, but I'm tired of approaching you and always being turned down.

I can't deal with it much longer."

Don's response is alarming to Mitsi.

"I'll cut back on my schedule,"

she says, thinking that her disinterest is 100% linked to her busy lifestyle.

Mitsi makes some adjustments, and for a while, the problems seem to disappear.

But soon, Mitsi realizes that now,

she's being intimate out of a sense of:

- **obligation,**

not

- **enthusiasm.**

Her once-healthy libido has **not** been revived.

There's a deeper issue that she can't quite see, clearly.

Through counseling, Mitsi discovers that:

— her libido dropped significantly after giving birth.

Parenting wore her out, and she was **annoyed** with Don for not helping more at home.

Her libido began to dwindle out of:

— exhaustion

and

— anger.

Her lack of interest in sex isn't just because she's "busy" — she's angry, too.

But that's only **part** of the problem — there's more.

"I also lost interest because I wasn't enjoying our lovemaking anymore," Mitsi says.

"Love-making had become routine. I was going through the motions to keep the peace.

I didn't know how to ask for what I wanted,

and

I didn't feel deserving of having my needs met."

After some self-reflection, Don realizes that:

— he's been ignoring Mitsi's needs

and

— focusing only on what he wants.

Together, Don and Mitsi make a new commitment:

- **to create an honest dialogue about their true feelings,**

- **to take care not to be overly-busy,**

and

- **to be creative**

and

- **to have fun**

as they **learn**

- **to become intimate again.**

At their final session, Don & Mitsi are feeling good.

The spark is growing brighter, and they're communicating openly.

*"We have **new priorities** now,"* says Mitsi.

*"Our relationship has **deepened**."*

ROB AND JUDY:

A story of rebirth.

When I first chatted with Rob and Judy, they had been committed to each other for five years.

They had not married but they intended to tie the knot in the future.

Their bond had been as **close** as two committed people could get.

That is until...

Judy found out that Rob had been intimate with someone else ... more than once.

Judy explained:

"When I first found out, I was devastated.

'How could he?' I thought.

'After all we meant to each other.'"

Then her **self-doubt** kicked in, relentlessly:

"It must be my fault, I must have done something wrong.

I'm not sexy enough."

Initially, Rob was a bit reluctant to discuss his infidelity.

But after a while, he let down his guard and explained that for quite some time, Judy had been so wrapped up in her work, that there was no time for their relationship.

"I reached out to Judy," he said.

"I told her I was lonely and craving affection and time with her.

She pretty much ignored my requests.

I know that part of it is cultural ... the way she was raised in another culture.

But I have needs too.

And then I met someone at work who gave me lots of attention, and made me feel good.

I felt attracted to her and things progressed until we were intimate."

This couple was sincerely willing to resolve the issues that had caused a rift between them.

But first, both needed to do some **individual personal growth work**:

Judy needed to resolve her:

— anger,

— sense of betrayal,

and

— self-doubt

because of Rob's affair.

Rob needed to:

— forgive himself for having the affair

and to :

— uncover why he felt a need to violate his commitment to Judy.

While Rob and Judy were working on themselves individually, they also worked with me as a couple, to:

- **strengthen** their communication skills

and to

- **define** their goals for their relationship.

Once they determined that they were on the same page in terms of what they wanted for their relationship, each was highly motivated to achieve these goals.

For Judy, that included:

- making sure that work didn't eat into precious relationship time.

She also realized that:

- the values that she learned about sex while growing up, weren't working for her;

  they were rigid and contributed to the rift that developed between her and Rob.

She focused on:

- **relaxing** more,

- letting sex be **fun**,

and

- expressing her **playful** side more.

A significant part of Rob's growth work focused on learning how to :

- **satisfy his own needs**,

instead of

- **looking "out there"** for gratification.

He also learned that just because he:

- feels a **physical** (or hormonal) hunger,

doesn't mean that he:

- needs to **act** on it.

Instead, he can:

- **enjoy** the physical sensation

and then,

- simply let it **subside**.

Today, this couple is:

- **loving,**

- **content,**

and

- **closer than ever.**

Both are grateful that they didn't allow the unfortunate sexual activity to destroy their relationship.

STEP 6

Release Expectations.

Once you start rekindling the **romance** and **intimacy** in your relationship, you might share an experience that is:

- **really super passionate ...**

and

- **very exciting.**

That experience might leave both of you thinking,

"Hooray!

Let's do exactly what we just did, every night, and try to replicate that experience.

We'll be all set, for life."

But...

- **Try to let go of any expectations about how things "should" be.**

The way your body responds to your partner's touch **today** might not be the same as:

— yesterday,

or

— tomorrow.

The things that excite you about your partner **today** might not be the same as:

— last Tuesday,

or

— next month.

Enjoy each other's touch, company and words, but...

- **try to release any expectations about what "needs" to happen or "should" happen when you kiss, touch, or are intimate.**

If one — or both — of you has an orgasm?

Great.

If neither of you has an orgasm?

Great (i.e., that's fine too!).

If all you do is massage each other's feet, laugh and cuddle?

Great.

If all you do is kiss each other's necks while you're making dinner together?

Great.

The more pressure you put on yourselves to "perform" or "respond" in a certain way, the less likely you are to have a good time.

Instead,

- **focus on honoring the new commitment you've written down (back in Step 4), and remember that any form of intimacy is a beautiful thing.**

Relax and enjoy.

WRAP UP

It Is Possible To Grow, and To Love Again.

When a relationship goes through a dry spell — without kissing, touching or sexual connection — it can feel **deeply stressful**.

And it's easy to feel **rejected**.

But when you bottle up those feelings inside, it makes it difficult to rebuild the kind of:

— relationship

and

— sex life

that you want.

It might take a little while to acclimate to **a new way of living** and **relating**:

- **taking the time** that you need to release negative feelings, safely and appropriately

  (like you learned in Step 2),

- **learning** how to ask for what you want

  (like you explored in Step 3),

- **creating time** for a special date night or pausing to kiss in the doorway before going to work

  (like you practiced in Step 5)

but it is possible…

- **to change old patterns,**

and

- **to create something new.**

That's one of the **most beautiful things about being human**.

We always have the capacity to evolve and improve.

To grow — and grow again.

To love — and love again.

MORE TIPS, MORE TOOLS

FAQs About Decreased Sex Drive — Causes and Fixes.

Now that you've read Steps 1 through Step 6 of this Life Guide, you know more about about why relationships can lose their "spark" — and how to change old patterns so that your relationship can grow. Here are even more tips and tools to continue your journey to create the relationship and intimacy that you desire.

Read on for my answers[3] to some of the more typical questions I've been asked over the past 3+ decades as I've helped people learn to rekindle the "spark" — and to grow and love again.

---

[3] The questions and answers are summarized here, to maximize your learning experience.

Question No. 1 — Lost interest in sex

Resolving Anger That Was Blocking Desire.

"I've been married for about a year. During the first few months, I enjoyed being sexually intimate with my husband. It was fun and pleasing.

But as he became increasingly comfortable with the "settled-in" feeling that we were having as a married couple, he started to show a side of himself that I'd never seen before... he started "playfully" teasing me about how short I am (I'm 5 ft, he's 6 ft 2").

At first I laughed it off, but then it started to bother me. I told him it made me uncomfortable and asked him to stop. He replied that he was just being playful and that he didn't mean any harm by doing that, but that he would stop.

He stopped the teasing for a few weeks... then it started up again — but now, when he teased me about my "short legs," he added a little tap on my leg with his hand. I noticed I was getting turned off from sex. I didn't want him to touch me. I thought it was because I was mad that he was teasing me and touching my leg... so I again asked him to stop teasing me, and touching me when he teased me. He stopped, mostly. Now and then, he teases and taps, but I know he doesn't mean to be mean to me, and he's trying to stop. So I thought I was "over" being mad about this.

In the last few months, again I've had no interest in sex. I thought it's because I'm working long hours, so I'm too tired to have sex. But I was never too tired in the past... and I liked having sex. I checked with my doctor - my health is fine. Could I still be mad about the teasing? Could that be what's wiping out my libido?"

Response:

Your questions appear to be right on the target.

Since you've ruled out the possibility of a physical cause for your fatigue (*"I'm too tired to have sex"*), it would make sense to explore the possibility that:

one or more emotion might be what's blocking your desire for sex.

Emotional blockage looks like a particularly likely candidate, because, based on the background information that you included with your questions, it appears that:

you tried to resolve your anger by reaching an INTELLECTUAL conclusion

*"...I **know** he doesn't mean to be mean to me, and he's trying to stop. So I **thought** I was "over" being mad about this."*

However,

you haven't yet directly addressed and, therefore, resolved the EMOTION (anger.)

Until the emotion itself is addressed and resolved,

it's conceivable that your unresolved anger is blocking your desire for intimacy.

[Note to reader:

*At this point in my response, I included a suggestion to start with a **writing exercise** to express those angry feelings using pen and paper.*

*The writing exercise that I suggested was similar to the one that you read about earlier in this Life Guide **(Step 1 Write down your feelings.)***

*I also suggested that the writing exercise be followed by an **exercise for emotional release**.*

*This exercise was similar to the one that you read about in Step 2 of this Life Guide. That Step was titled, **"Release negative feelings ... safely."***

If you feel that this would be a good time to refresh your memory about the contents of Step 1 and Step 2, please go back to those pages in this Life Guide now.

Why pause your reading of this Life Guide for a review of previously-read material?

Because:

*Step 1 and Step 2 are **vital building blocks** to begin to lay the foundation to get your relationship back on track... and then better than ever!*

Once you've you've done your review, then come back to these FAQs, and pick up with Question No. 2.]

Question No. 2 — Not OK to say "No"

Learning To Trust Your Body's Cues.

My partner and I are both very busy, but somehow, he always has energy to be intimate. As for me, there are times when I'm just plain tired! During those times, all my body wants to do is rest.

The thing is... I know what a demanding schedule my partner keeps, and since he's never too tired for sex, I'm wondering if there's something wrong with me during those times when I just want to curl up in bed and go to sleep.

He says he's fine with that, and that he understands... and I take him at his word, but I worry that our relationship with deteriorate if I "go to sleep" too often — but I really am tired.

Another version of what I worry about happened just last weekend. I was in the shower. He then followed me into the shower, and started to pleasure my body (He had already taken a shower, by the way.) It was a lovely experienced and I liked it a lot. But then, I had had enough... I wasn't tired or rushing to go somewhere (e.g., work), I'd simply had enough.

Of course, he wanted to continue, but when I said, in response, that I enjoyed our sharing very much, but that I wanted to get out of shower, he was completely OK with that.

The problem was that I felt so guilty (and afraid that he would lose interest if I didn't stay in the shower and continue our pleasure), that even though I did get out of the shower when I said I wanted to, I felt guilty for the rest of the day. Why didn't I want to stay in the shower and continue to enjoy my partner? Where did my sexual drive go?

Response:

First, with regards to sexual intimacy, it's wonderful that you had such a positive experience in the shower.

As to your reasons for not wanting to stay in the shower and continue to enjoy your partner, from an **emotional standpoint,** this sounds like a classic example of being our own worst enemy.

Why?

Because instead of:

— **accepting** your body's natural cues

("I've had enough, I'm more than satisfied, thank you.");

your inner critic took over and was:

— **judging** you

("What's wrong with me? Where did my sexual drive go?)

and

— **scaring** you

("He'll lose interest if you leave the shower before he wants to.")

Of course, it's always wise to check with a qualified medical physician, to rule out any possible physical reasons for low, or no, sexual drive.

That said, it's not a good idea to:

Ignore our body's natural cues

or to:

Allow **self-judgment** and **fear** to motivate our choics.

The first lesson here could be:

- **Trust my body.**

- **Trust my body's cues.**

The second lesson here could be:

- **Trust my partner's acceptance of me and my choices.**

- **Trust that I deserve a partner who accepts me and my choices.**

With those lessons in place, guilt feelings don't stand a chance.

Question No. 3 — No sex for sex's sake

Prioritizing Self-Respect Over Keeping the Peace.

"I enjoy sex with my wife, but she always wants it, and I'm not always up to it, physically. That's because my job is in construction, and it's very physically demanding.

When I tell my wife, "Not tonight honey, I'd love to but I'm exhausted," she gets very angry. Then she pouts, and that's usually followed by a few days of giving me the silent treatment. I think she thinks I don't love her if I don't have sex with her (even though I've told her over and over again, that I do love her, and that has nothing to do with how many times we have sex.)

On top of that, when I am rested and I indicate that I'm interested in being intimate with her, without fail, she always says, "No." It's like she's punishing me for having declined to have sex in the past, during those times that I was legitimately physically exhausted.

Now, we don't have much sex at all and she's convince herself that I have a problem with my sex drive. According to my internist at my most recent physical, "everything" is working just fine!

So now, I don't know which direction to go in...

(a) Force myself to have sex with her when I'm too tired — just to appease her;

or

(b) Don't just have sex for sex's sake, and be willing to put up with her silent treatment for days?

Response:

Thank you for sharing.

If I may take the liberty of adding a third option to the two choices that you laid out in your question, in terms of which direction to go in, here's how option (c) might read:

"or

(c) Maintain my self-respect

(meaning that I don't have sex with my wife for the wrong reasons — to avoid her silent treatment).

- **There is no price that can be put on self-respect. It's that valuable... and that precious.**

When self-respect is intact, then somehow everything seems more:

— manageable

— tolerable

and

— doable.

Some people have even found that getting "the silent treatment" is more bearable, when their integrity is intact, and they had chosen not to "sell out" on themselves or their values, in order to avoid the wall of silence.

That said, this is a deeply personal decision to make, in terms of which option to choose.

As you contemplate the best course of action to take, it's wise to do some:

- **introspection**

and

- **self-reflection.**

This way, you're laying the ground work for **tuning into your own inner wisdom** — your own inner guidance system, that, when you listen:

— **clearly**

and

— **closely enough,**

can **reveal** to you the uniquely personal answer that you seek.

WHAT'S NEXT?

Resources... To Keep the "Spark" Shining.

This Life Guide is "technically" complete, but I wanted to give you some **more resources on partnerships, stress-management and self-care** ... in case you'd like to keep the "spark" shining.

Here are some of my favorites — articles I've authored,[4] books I've written, and inspiring insights that I shared when I was interviewed by a reporter from the Weekend Today Show, to savor at your leisure.

Enjoy to the fullest!

---

[4] Except where otherwise noted, all articles referenced in this section were published online.

PARTNERSHIPS

The Love Tune-Up: How to Amp Up the Love That's Naturally Inside You to Enjoy Happy, Healthy Relationships — A 14-Day Course That Can Change Your Life
— Written by Dr. Suzanne Gelb, PhD.

I created *The Love Tune-Up* because healthy love is the answer to every problem, in one way or another. Everyone has the capacity to find deep reserves of self-love, within. In order to create the relationship of your dreams with another person, first, you need to create the relationship of your dreams with yourself.

With this 14-day course, you'll have access to 14 short lessons (and a few more surprises!) to help you tune-up and upgrade your relationship with yourself. The lessons in *The Love Tune-Up* can work wonders for couples.

https://amzn.to/2XQ7190

Real Men Don't Vacuum. And Other Misguided Myths That Cause Conflict in Relationships
— Written by Dr. Suzanne Gelb, PhD.

I wrote this handbook decades ago (published in 1991, by National Seminars Publications, Inc.), but the information within its pages is timeless.

Topics addressed include: the havoc that unrealistic expectations can wreak on relationships, how to break down barriers to effective communication, and how to constructively minimize tension in a marriage [applies to other relationships, as well] for example — all this, set against a backdrop of dispelling marital myths such as:

"Having a Child Can Solve Marital Problems" and "True Lovers Automatically Know Each Other's Thoughts and Feelings".

https://www.amazon.com/Real-Men-Dont-Vacuum-Gelb/dp/B000E5CWWA

Spring Cleaning for Your Life [Part 2/3]
— Published on The Huffington Post.

This article is part of a series on tidying up our inner world – I call this "Spring Cleaning for your life." It contains a checklist for couples that can add some sizzle and tender closeness to their relationship.

Topics on the checklist: "Goals and life direction," "Sex and intimacy," "Forgiveness" and "Self-love."

https://www.huffpost.com/entry/spring-cleaning-for-your-life-part-2-3_n_7271136

How to Succeed Everywhere: 10 Tips for Balance at Work, Home, in Relationships
— Written by Shelby Marra, published online on NBC's Today.

Learn my top ten tips on how women [can apply to anyone] can become high achievers in whatever they do — at work, in romance and as a parent.

For partners, the romance section in this article, can be especially insightful.

https://www.today.com/health/how-become-high-achieving-woman-work-your-relationship-parent-t33071

Side note: As my colleague, friend, and gifted writing teacher, Alex Franzen said: *"THIS IS AMAZING! Being interviewed by a reporter from NBC's Today Show? Uh, that's the big leagues!"*

Yes, that's what happened. Shelby Marra with NBC's Today Show in New York, requested an interview with me so that she could write this article featuring me, for TODAY.com's Successful Women series.

How To Forgive The One Who Hurt You Most Of All (A Life Guide)
— Written by Dr. Suzanne Gelb, Ph.D, J.D.

If you are feeling weighed down by grief or anger from past fights or betrayals, and want to learn how to forgive, this guide could be a perfect fit.

https://amzn.to/31qPCGq

What Readers of Dr. Gelb's Life Guide are Saying:

"I was quite excited to receive your Forgiveness Life Guide and hoped it would help me in healing a particularly intense issue I've been harboring for many years. So far, nothing has worked and I was beyond ready to get this poison out of my life.

This past weekend, I read and thoroughly completed your guide. It was a definite "Aha moment" for me. I felt a tangible, immediate shift in my thinking.

This is no joke nor is it an exaggeration but I now feel more energy, clarity, and excitement than I've felt in ages. (think puppy after a bath) And I'm no longer afraid that the feelings of betrayal might be triggered and resurface because I know I have your guide to get me right back on track.

It was so simple and yet so powerful. I can't begin to thank you enough."

—Beth

"I didn't want to let go of my grudge against my dad, but holding onto it was stressful. This Guide helped me to understand that letting go of my grudge and being forgiving was for ME, not necessarily for my dad. That was liberating.

Dr. Gelb's Guide also helped me stop denying & ignoring my feelings. By feeling, instead of pushing my feelings down (only to later come back up), I felt in charge—instead of somehow controlled by—my feelings."

—Dave

"This Guide lifted the weight of the world from my shoulders.

I was consumed by my anger towards my ex ... until I read this guide. Now I have released my anger (safely), and I'm at peace. I am so grateful to you."

—Terry

"This guidebook has shown me the difference between natural, healthy, appropriate anger ... and the heavy weight of a grudge. I'm glad that now I know the difference."

—Alexandra Franzen, Published Author, Writing Teacher

You Want Couple's Counseling But Your Partner Does Not
— Published in Dr. Gelb's column, "All Grown Up," on Psychology Today.

Does this mean you should give up? Not necessarily. In this article, you can learn why your seeking counseling, even if your partner does not, can be of benefit to you, and possibly be positive for your current relationship as well.

https://www.psychologytoday.com/us/blog/all-grown/201504/you-want-couple-s-counseling-your-partner-does-not

What Really Happens in a Therapy Session?
— Published in Dr. Gelb's column, "All Grown Up," on Psychology Today.

Ever wonder how a therapy session works? 196,083 people have been wondering - they viewed my article on this subject. Topics covered in the article include: Choosing the right therapist, effectiveness of in-person therapy vs. phone or video format, and the value of seeing a therapist vs. talking to friends or family.

https://www.psychologytoday.com/intl/blog/all-grown/201512/what-really-happens-in-therapy-session

Why I Still Believe People Can Change
— Published on Positively Positive.

Over the course of decades of working in the field of emotional wellness, I've seen so many people release negative emotions and embrace love. That's why I believe people can change… even someone who had a real problem with jealousy (something that can destroy relationships), but learned to strengthen her self-worth and be free of resentment. Read this article to learn more.

http://www.positivelypositive.com/2014/12/15/why-i-still-believe-that-people-can-change/

STRESS-MANAGEMENT

If You Want to Make Tomorrow Less Stressful—Start Tonight
— Published in Dr. Gelb's Column, "Be Well At Work," on The Muse.

The stress management tips that I cover in this article, apply to all aspects of life, not just a workday. That said, parenting is one of the most important "jobs."

This article is a relevant read if you want to learn how to manage your emotions and keep your stress levels in check.

It includes suggestions for stress-relieving activities that take place after-work and an empowering morning affirmation to set the tone for a positive day. You'll also learn about the importance of scheduling deep breathing breaks during the day, and how to do an emotional inventory (and an emotional release, if needed) at the end of the day.

https://www.themuse.com/advice/if-you-want-to-make-tomorrow-less-stressfulstart-tonight

Side note: The Muse is an online platform that attracts more than 75 million people each year, to help them be at the top of their game at work.

I'm honored to have received the praise below, from Adrian Granzella Larssen, Editor-in-Chief, in response to an article that I wrote for The Muse:

"Wow! This is fantastic stuff. You're clearly incredible at what you do, and I'm so thrilled to share your advice with our audience!"

Stressed Out at Work? How to Cope — Without Turning to Food or Booze.
— Originally published on The Huffington Post.

Workplace demands and pressure seems to "come with the territory" in so many instances.

It's no surprise then, that many people routinely try to "escape" this stress by consuming something sweet [lots of it! — say, a pint of ice cream], numbing out with alcohol, or some other pacifier.

A far healthier approach would be to manage work-related stress by relying on one's inner strength. To learn more, including my five stress relief techniques, this article is a must-read.

https://www.huffpost.com/entry/stressed-out-at-work-how_n_6711034

Don't Feel Like Exercising? 3 Steps To Get You Off The Couch
— Published in Dr. Gelb's column, "All Grown Up," on Psychology Today.

We know how good it feels AFTER we've worked out. The problem for many people though, is GETTING MOTIVATED to work out. Sometimes, unresolved emotions "weigh" us down, and dull our desire to work out.

This article offers tips on how to begin to clear out some of the emotional weight that can stop us dead in our tracks, and keep our running shoes in the closet… instead of on our feet!

https://www.psychologytoday.com/blog/all-grown/201505/don-t-feel-exercising-3-steps-get-you-the-couch

5 Ways to Stop Yourself from Eating When You're not Hungry.
— Originally published on Psych Central.

In addition to believing in yourself and your ability to handle life's challenges without the illusory "help" of food [or whatever person, place, or thing, someone might turn to as a coping mechanism], in this article I also lay out five strategies to consider implementing, in am effort to thwart using food [or any addictive substance/ behavior for that matter] to cope.

Strategies include: Identifying the real source of hunger (clue: it's not physical), dialoguing with the food, and remembering the downside of eating for the wrong reasons… disappointment afterwards, and physical discomfort.

https://psychcentral.com/blog/5-ways-to-stop-yourself-from-eating-when-youre-not-hungry/

How to Find Work That You Love When You're Stuck in a Job That You Hate (A Life Guide)
— Created by Dr. Suzanne Gelb, Ph.D., J.D.

Inside this Life Guide, you'll find steps that can help you to discover and create your ideal career.

Topics that are covered include: clarifying your true aspirations in life (they might not be what you think!), discovering your career desires and non-negotiable "dealbreakers," managing fear and job-hunt rejection, dealing with procrastination, building confidence, and more!

https://amzn.to/2YmrFO2

Feeling Phone-verwhelmed? 5 Tips To Help You Create A Healthier, Happier Relationship With Your Smartphone
— Published in Dr. Gelb's column, "All Grown Up," on Psychology Today.

Are you one of those people who loves your phone and everything that it enables you to do (what a timesaver it can be!), but it's become so much a part of your life that you feel a bit burnt out and sometimes long for more simplicity (maybe even a time when smartphones weren't invented yet!)?

This article lays out 5 suggested steps to create a healthier relationship with your phone… a relationship that has more balance. The steps can be applied to any type of technology that you're involved with, not just your phone.

https://www.psychologytoday.com/blog/all-grown/201508/feeling-phone-verwhelmed

SELF-CARE

You Are The Best Investment You'll Ever Make
— Published in Dr. Gelb's column, "All Grown-Up," on Psychology Today.

In this article, I address ways to invest in ourselves and I present some questions about self-investment practices that readers can reflect on.

Readers are encouraged to make a list of doable ways they can invest in themselves. I offer suggestions about what to include on their list.

https://www.psychologytoday.com/blog/all-grown/201511/you-are-the-best-investment-youll-ever-make

6 Self-Sabotaging Habits You Need To Drop Right Now
— Published on Mind Body Green.

In this article, I encourage readers to do a "habit audit." This means: Paying attention to whether they're sabotaging themselves by being mean to themselves, saying "Yes" when they really mean "No," or blaming their parents for how their life turned out for example,… and to drop these habits if they're present.

https://www.mindbodygreen.com/0-14014/6-selfsabotaging-habits-you-need-to-drop-right-now.html

The Greatest Cheerleader One Can Have — Lives Within: How to Stay Strong When Not Everyone is Cheering For Our Success

— Published in Dr. Gelb's column, "All Grown Up" on Psychology Today.

This article tells the story of a personal experience that I had, where a stranger projected their own negativity towards me.

Although initially, the experience was unsettling, followed by mild annoyance and a passing moment of sadness, it served as a reminder that not everyone is cheering for our success (whether you're wanting to launch a business, sell your home, change jobs, etc.)

But that's ok because we can be own greatest cheerleader and stay true to our vision, no matter what. Read the article to learn more.

https://www.psychologytoday.com/us/blog/all-grown/201902/the-greatest-cheerleader-person-can-have-lives-within

How Successful People Do More in 24 Hours Than the Rest of Us Do in a Week
— Published on Newsweek; also published on The Muse

The content in this article is bound to inspire. Some of the topics I cover include: "Fully Commit," "Ban 'Friendly Interruptions' at All Costs." "Hang With Fellow Super-Achievers," and "Prevent Emotions From Building."

It takes a self-loving person, who prioritizes self-care, to take this type of positive action to further their success.

https://www.newsweek.com/career/how-successful-people-do-more-24-hours-rest-us-do-week

Why "Certain People" Make Us Feel Completely Insane And How To Reclaim Our "Zen."
— Published on Positively Positive.

If you've ever felt really mad when you're around a particular person (you know, the type of anger that can stick around for hours, even when you're no longer in the presence of the person whom you're angry at), this article might be worth a read.

Relationships can be important teachers, bringing to our attention, for example, emotions that we're experiencing that need to be resolved.

That's the focus of this article — how to handle our anger when someone makes us feel annoyed… but where our annoyance is excessive given the situation at hand. I include three questions, along with answers, that can be helpful for people who want to replace being mad around certain people with reclaiming their "zen."

https://bit.ly/2HOCdAg

Welcome Home: Release Addictions and Return to Love
— — Written by Dr. Suzanne Gelb, Ph.D, J.D.

If you're wanting to break free from an addictive habit (from alcoholism to workaholic-ism) and connect to your essence — love — that's what this book is about.

A core message in *Welcome Home* is that with patience and courage, it's possible to learn how to become emotionally self-reliant. That means depending on ourselves, not some external substance, activity, or person, to manage our challenges, and to feel at peace and at home in our lives.

https://amzn.to/2vwXmIa

"Just Believe." How I Learned To Trust In The Universe, Even When All Hope Seemed Lost
— Published in Positively Positive.

This is a true and inspiring article about the importance of believing in yourself … and keeping hope alive … even when the future looks bleak.

http://www.positivelypositive.com/2015/03/26/just-believe-how-i-learned-to-trust-in-the-universe-even-when-all-hope-seemed-lost/

ABOUT THE AUTHOR

Dr. Suzanne Gelb, Ph.D., J.D. is a psychologist, life coach, TV commentator and author. For 3+ decades, she has helped couples learn to rekindle the "spark" in their relationships — to grow and love again, using tools like the ones in this book.

Dr. Gelb's inspiring insights on emotional wellness have been featured on more than 200 radio programs, 260 TV interviews, and online on Time, Newsweek, Forbes, Psychology Today, The Huffington Post, NBC's Today, and many more.

She is the author of several other books on relationships including **The Love Tune-Up: How to Amp Up the Love That's Naturally Inside You to Enjoy Happy, Healthy Relationships — A 14-Day Course That Can Change Your Life**, **How To Forgive The One Who Hurt You Most Of All**, and **Real Men Don't Vacuum. And Other Misguided Myths That Cause Conflict in Relationships**.

Dr. Gelb believes that it is never too late to become the person — and partner — you want to be. Strong. Confident. Calm. Creative. Free of all of the burdens that have held you back — no matter what happened in the past.

OTHER BOOKS BY THE AUTHOR

The Love Tune-Up: How to Amp Up the Love That's Naturally Inside You to Enjoy Happy, Healthy Relationships. (A 14-Day Course)

How to Forgive the One Who Hurt You Most. (A Life Guide)

Real Men Don't Vacuum. And Other Misguided Myths That Cause Conflict in Relationships.

How to Deal With People Who Drive You Absolutely Nuts. (A Life Guide)

Welcome Home: Release Addiction and Return to Love.

How To Care for Yourself — When You're A Caregiver For Someone Else. (A Life Guide)

How to Reach Your Ideal Weight Through Kindness, Not Craziness. (A Life Guide)

How to Find Work That You Love When You're Stuck in a Job That You Hate. (A Life Guide)

How To Navigate Being Single — And Savor Your Dating Adventure. (A Life Guide)

It Starts With You – How To Raise Happy, Successful Children By Becoming the Best Role-Model You Can Possibly Be. A Guidebook For Parents.

How to Get Your Kids to Cooperate and Help Them Become the Best Grown-Ups They Can Be. (A Life Guide)

Helping Your Teen Make Healthy Choices About Dating and Intimacy. (A Life Guide)

How To Get Ready To Be a Parent — and Be the Best Mom or Dad You Can Possibly Be. (A Life Guide)

Aging With Grace, Strength and Self-Love. (A Life Guide)

INDEX[5]

A

absence of physical contact, 4
allow self-judgment and fear, 77
an exercise for emotional release, 16, 74

B

be seen at your best, 49

C

change old patterns, 70, 71

E

emotional and lifestyle aspects, 7
emotional blockage, 73
emotional release, 16, 19, 74, 87
emotional relief, 20

F

feel(ing) connected, 5, 47
feeling strong emotions, 21
finding the real issues, 57

G

going through the motions to keep the peace, 59

H

happy endings, 51

I

individual personal growth work, 62
introspection, 80
investing time, energy and love, 37

---

[5] The page numbers in this index refer to the printed version of this book.

L

lack of/lost interest in sex, 3, 59, 72
learning to trust your body's cues, 75
libido, 3, 6, 7, 24, 58, 72
lose the/their spark, 23, 71
loss of desire, 3, 6

M

maintain my self-respect, 79
my partner's acceptance of me, 77

N

nourish and improve, 1, 8

P

partnership, 81, 82
pent-up, negative emotions, 20
pent-up feelings, 6, 20, 22
pent-up unresolved feelings, 9
physical intimacy, 3, 4
physiological factors, 7
pillow-pounding exercise, 18, 20, 21
pounding exercise, 19, 20
put your words into action, 36

R

"rejection", 4
rekindle that "spark", 1, 8, 71, 95
rekindling the spark, 56
rekindling the romance and intimacy, 66
release (any) expectations, 66, 67
release negative feelings ... safely, 15, 70, 74
roommate(s), 20, 57
"roommate" situation, 24

S

savor this special milestone, 35
say what you want, 23
saying what you really WANT to say, 25
self-care, 81, 91
self-judgment and fear, 77
self-reflection, 59, 80
self-respect, 78, 79
silent treatment, 78, 79
solo date, 45, 46
spark, 1, 8, 23, 28, 36, 51, 55, 56, 60, 71, 81, 95
speak from your heart, 25
stress-management, 81, 87

T

things you are NOT going to
   do, 30
to create something new, 70
trust my body/trust my body's
   cues, 77

U

ultimate fantasy list, 41

V

"venting zone", 20
vital building blocks, 74

W

what do you want?, 25
what "emotional relief" feels
   like, 20
what you WILL do, 32
write down your feelings, 9
write a new commitment, 29
writing down a new
   commitment, 36

Y

your own inner wisdom, 80

www.ingramcontent.com/pod-product-compliance
Lightning Source LLC
Chambersburg PA
CBHW020143130526
44591CB00030B/197